P9-DCS-059

Accounting Workbook

An Introduction to Accounting

Jackie Stachiw
&
Brandon Williams

Accounting Workbook: An Introduction to Accounting

Copyright 2015

All rights reserved

Printed in the United States of America

Published by SM&DS through Createspace Independent Publishing Platform

ISBN-13: 978-1515217220

ISBN-10: 1515217221

Table of Contents

Lesson 1: Accounting Basics with Vocabulary

Instructions: Match the word with its correct definition.

Exercise 1

1) ____ A law implemented to reduce unethical corporate behavior	A. Sole Proprietorship
2) ____ An information system that records and communicates economic events of an organization	B. Partnership
3) ____ Company's legal debts	C. Corporation
4) ____ A business owned by two or more people	D. Accounting
5) ____ The owners' claim to assets	E. Sarbanes Oxley Act
6) ____ A business owned by 1 person	F. Assets
7) ____ A business organized as a legal entity owned by stockholders	G. Liabilities
8) ____ Resources owned by a business	H. Stockholder's Equity

Exercise 2

1) ____ Money owed by a business	A. Common Stock
2) ____ The right to receive money in the future	B. Dividends
3) ____ A cost that arises as part of a business's operating activities	C. Inventory
4) ____ Cash payments to stockholders	D. Accounts Receivable
5) ____ Goods available for future sale	E. Accounts Payable
6) ____ Ownership in a corporation	F. Expenses

Exercise 3

1) ____Management's explanation of how a business has performed in the past, its current ability to function, and its outlook	A. Income Statements
2) ____Includes financial statements, management discussions, notes, and independent auditor's report	B. Retained Earnings Statement
3) ____Shows how much of previous income was distributed or retained in a business to allow for growth	C. Balance Sheet
4) ____Reports revenue and expenses during a period of time	D. Statement of Cash Flows
5) ____These clarify financial statements and provide detail	E. Annual Reports
6) ____A formal opinion that reports if a company's financial statements comply with GAAP	F. Management Discussion and Analysis
7) ____Reports what a business owns and owes at a point in time	G. Notes
8) ____Reports inflows and outflows of cash over a period of time	H. Auditor's Report

Exercise 4

1) ____A company's obligations that are due within the operating cycle or one year	A. Current Assets
2) ____Assets with no physical substance, but valuable in today's marketplace	B. Property, Plant, Equipment,
3) ____Obligations that a company will pay after one year or operating cycle	C. Intangible Assets
4) ____Assets that a company expects to convert to cash or use up within the operating cycle or one year	D. Current Liabilities
5) ____Investments of assets into the business	E. Long Term Liabilities
6) ____Assets with long useful lives that are currently used in operations	F. Common Stock

Exercise 5

1) ___ Expenses paid in cash before they are used	A. Adjusting Entries
2) ___ Journal entries that convert records to the accrual basis of accounting	B. Deferrals
3) ___ When a company receives money for a service that it has not yet performed	C. Prepaid Expense
4) ___ Process of allocating the cost of an asset to expense over its life	D. Depreciation
5) ___ Shows the balance of all the adjusted accounts at the end of the accounting period	E. Unearned Revenue
6) ___ Expenses incurred but not yet paid or recorded at the statement date	F. Accrued Revenues
7) ___ Revenues for services performed but not recorded at the statement date	G. Accrued Expenses
8) ___ Costs or revenues that are recognized later than the point when the cash was initially exchanged	H. Adjusted Trial Balance

Exercise 6

1) ___ Assumes that the earliest goods purchased are the first to be sold	A. Just In Time Inventory
2) ___ Allocates cost of goods sold on the basis of a weighted average	B. Specific Identification Method
3) ___ Assumes that the latest goods purchased are the first to be sold	C. First In, First Out
4) ___ Companies that keep records of the original cost of each individual item	D. Last In, First Out
5) ___ Inventory is stated at the lower of either its cost or market value as determined by its replacement cost	E. Average Cost
6) ___ A Company holds the goods of other parties and tries to sell them but does not take ownership	F. Lower Cost or Market
7) ___ Companies manufacture or purchase goods just in time for use	G. Consigned Goods

Exercise 7

1) _____ The sale of bonds above face value	A. Convertible Bonds
2) _____ Bonds that can be converted into common stock at the holder's option	B. Callable Bonds
3) _____ Date that the final payment is due to the investor	C. Bond Certificate
4) _____ Bonds that the issuer can redeem at a stated dollar amount prior to the maturity date	D. Face Value
5) _____ Equivalent amount today	E. Present Value
6) _____ Amount of principal due at maturity	F. Maturity Date
7) _____ Issued to the investor to provide evidence of the investor's claim against a company	G. Premium

Exercise 8

1) _____ Assets, liabilities, and equity accounts that appear on the balance sheet	A. Event
2) _____ The book containing accounts	B. Transaction
3) _____ List of all open accounts in the ledger with their balances	C. Real Accounts
4) _____ Revenue, expense, and dividends accounts	D. Nominal Accounts
5) _____ The book of original entry where the company first records transactions	E. Ledger
6) _____ A happening of consequence	F. Journal
7) _____ An external event involving the transfer or exchange between two or more entities	G. Trial Balance

Exercise 9

1) _____ Amount of equity interest in a subsidiary not attributable to the parent company	A. Operating Section
2) _____ Section of income statement which reports the revenues and expenses of a company	B. Non-Operating Section
3) _____ Calculated as the net income divided by the average outstanding common shares and must be disclosed	C. Income Tax
4) _____ Report of revenues and expenses that resulted from secondary activities of the company	D. Discontinued Operations
5) _____ Reports federal and states taxes levied on income from continuing operations in an income statement	E. Extraordinary Items
6) _____ Material gains or losses resulting from the disposition of a component of the company	F. Non-Controlling Interest
7) _____ Unusual and infrequent gains and losses	G. Earnings Per Share

Exercise 10

1) _____ Translates a company's mission and strategy into a set of performance measures that help implement strategy	A. Strategy
2) _____ Fundamental rethinking and redesign of business processes	B. Product Differentiation
3) _____ An organization's ability to offer products or services perceived by the customers to be superior and unique	C. Cost Leadership
4) _____ Actual production is less than what is optimal	D. Reengineering
5) _____ Reduction of a company's work force	E. Balanced Scorecard
6) _____ How an organization matches its own capacities with the opportunities in the marketplace to accomplish its objectives	F. Unused Capacity
7) _____ An organization's ability to achieve lower costs relative to competitors	G. Downsizing

Exercise 11

1) _____ Beginning Inventory + Purchases – Ending Inventory=	A. Interest Revenue
2) _____ Inventory cost flow assumption under which the ending inventory would consist of the oldest purchase costs	B. A Contra Account
3) _____ A group of accounts which would be closed at the end of a fiscal period	C. Purchase Discount
4) _____ Inventory cost flow assumption which would result in the oldest purchase costs being included in cost of goods sold	D. Temporary Accounts
5) _____ Accrued interest on a note receivable	E. LIFO
6) _____ 365 divided by inventory turnover ratio	F. Cost of Goods Sold
7) _____ Sales returns and allowances	G. Gross Profit
8) _____ Net sales – cost of goods sold =	H. Adjusted Trial Balance
9) _____ Reduction in the amount to be paid by the buyer for prompt payment	I. Days in Inventory
10) _____ A list of account balances from which the financial statements should be prepared	J. FIFO

Lesson 2: Journal Entries

Instructions: Journalize the transactions.

1. The following transactions in August were as follows:

August 4-Collected $5,670 in cash from May 30th accounts receivable

August 5-Received $3,970 in cash for services provided

August 7-Purchased supplies on account for $1,020

August 9-Paid employee salaries of $4,480

August 12-Paid creditors $2,960 of accounts payable

August 14-Collected service fees in advance for $1,740

August 17-Received a bill for the utilities for $580

August 23-Billed customers for services provided for $2,810

August 26-Paid $600 for rent (One third covers August and the remainder covers the next two months)

August 31-Paid a cash dividend of $990 (First time dividends have been declared)

2. Nanu Inc. is a furniture retailer and uses the perpetual inventory system. During November, Nanu completed the following merchandising transactions:

Nov. 2 Purchased merchandise on account from Williams Co. $10,700, terms 1/10, n/30

Nov. 4 Sold merchandise on account $16,000, terms 2/10, n/30. The cost of the merchandise sold was $8,700.

Nov. 5 Paid freight of $800 on the Nov. 4 sale

Nov. 6 Received credit from Williams Co. for merchandise returned, $1,400 (Nov. 2 Purchase)

Nov. 11 Paid Williams Co. in full, less the discount

Prepare journal entries on the books of Nanu Inc. to record each of these transactions (only dates necessary, no explanation required).

3. On June 15th 2015, Kevin Smith filed for corporate status in the state of Missouri. The articles authorized 250,000 shares of common stock. The corporation was named 'Smith Inc.' On December 31, 2015, the transactions included the following:

A. On December 14th, an investor bought 500 shares of common stock for $100,000.

B. On December 19th, Kevin Smith purchased a van for his family. The cost of the car was $26,789 and the license, taxes, etc. were $934. He paid cash for all these items.

C. On December 29th, Smith arranged a loan by issuing a note for $60,000, with a requirement that the money was to be transferred to Smith's account early on December 31st. Smith was required to pay $400 a month interest (due on the last day of each month starting next year) and the $60,000 was to be paid off by December 31, 2016.

D. On December 31, Smith Inc. paid $139,000 to its manufacturer for devices that were delivered the same day. These inventory items will be sold to distributors in the future.

4. The Williams Corporation is a well-established company. The following transactions took place in March 2015.

A. Williams Corporation sold $378,000 worth of merchandise during the month. Of this amount, $261,000 was received in cash and the remainder on account.

B. Williams incurred expenses of $30,189 that related to selling, general, and administrative items. Of these, $18,022 was paid in cash and the remainder on account.

C. Williams paid dividends of $6,034 to the shareholders.

D. Williams paid cash of $123,004 to its research and development consultants for a new product under consideration. This transaction is considered as an R&D transaction.

5. Dar Inc. exchanged old equipment and $10,000 cash for equipment owned by Kitty Inc.

Below is information about the asset exchanged by Dar Inc. Assume the transaction has commercial substance. Journalize the transaction.

	Cost	Accumulated Depreciation	Book Value	Fair Value
Dar's Equipment	$250,000	$150,000	$100,000	$105,000

6. The Zuehlke Company was incorporated on January 1, 2014 with an initial capital of 10,000 shares of common stock having a $15 par value. The following transactions took place in January:

January 2: Office supplies costing $3,509 were purchased on account

January 3: $18,000 was paid as an advance for three months' rent

January 7: Provided services to its customers and received $28,000 in cash

January 11: Received $15,000 as an advance payment from customers

January 17: Paid wages to its employees for $3900

January 22: Received telephone bill of $844

7. We are following Mike around for the first few months as he starts his barbecue food chain called "Mike's Barbecue." Here are the events that took place.

On January 1st, Mike finds a nice building to put his restaurant in and signs a lease for $600 a month.

On January 8th, Mike takes out a loan to renovate his restaurant for $75,000 and agrees to pay back $1,000 a month. He spends the entire loan on improving the building's looks.

On January 11th, Mike buys $2,000 worth of supplies on account from vendors. He agrees to pay $250 a month.

On January 25th, the store opens up for business. In 5 days, Mike makes $15,020 in sales.

On February 1st, Mike's first rent payment is due.

On February 6th, Mike pays his employees $2,098 for their work.

On February 8th, Mike pays for an electric bill costing $340 and his first payment from his January 8th loan is also due.

On February 11th, Mike's first vendor inventory payment is due.

Lesson 3: Multiple Choice and True/False On Basic Material

1. A company pays for inventory within the cash discount period and receives the discount. This action will increase the gross profit percentage on these units when they are sold.
    a. True
    b. False

    Use the following information for questions 2 to 4: Stachiw Corporation (whose fiscal year ends on December 31) signed a 1 year note payable in the amount of $8000 on October 1, 2015. The note requires interest at an annual rate of 6%, principal and interest to be paid on the maturity date (November 30, 2016).

2. The amount of interest accrued on December 31, 2015 on the books of Stachiw Corp. is:
    a. $320
    b. $120
    c. $480
    d. $120

3. The adjusting entry for this accrued interest on the books of Stachiw Corp. on December 31, 2015 would be:
    a. Debit: Interest expense and Credit: Interest payable
    b. Debit: Interest receivable and Credit: Interest revenue
    c. Debit: Note payable and Credit: Cash
    d. Debit: Interest payable and Credit: Interest revenue

4. The correct entry on the books of Stachiw Corp. on October 1, 2015 would:
    a. Increase net income
    b. Decrease net income
    c. Decrease total assets
    d. Have no effect total income
    e. All of the above

5. The payment of a pre-existing accounts payable:
    a. Increases net income
    b. Decreases net income
    c. Has no effect on net income
    d. All of the above

6. On the income statement for a service business (such as an advertising agency), an amount referred to as gross profit would not be reported.
   a. True
   b. False

7. The Cook Apartments, Inc. collected one year of rent in advance on May 1, 2015 totaling $9,000 and recorded the collection as a liability. If their fiscal year ends on December 31, the revenue to be reported for 2015 would be:
   a. $5,600
   b. $6,000
   c. None of the above

8. Goods are shipped by the Williams Company on December 16, 2015, FOB destination. These goods are received by Williams' customer December 26, 2015. The goods should be included in Williams' ending inventory on December 31, 2015.
   a. True
   b. False

9. Stachiw's Dry Cleaners follows the revenue recognition principle. On October 4 a customer drops off laundry for cleaning. The cleaning is completed on October 7. On November 1 the customer picks up the clothing. When should Stachiw show that the revenue was earned?
   a. October 4
   b. October 7
   c. November 1
   d. None of the above

10. On March 1, 2015, Smith Corporation paid $48,000 cash for equipment that will be used in business operations. The equipment will be used for four years. Smith records depreciation expense of $9,000 for the calendar year ending December 31, 2015. Which accounting principle has been violated?
    a. Matching principle
    b. Depreciation principle
    c. Expense recognition principle
    d. No principle has been violated

11. Smith Company sells merchandise on account for $1,500 to Stachiw Company with credit terms of 2/10, n/30. Stachiw Company returns $400 of merchandise that was damaged, along with cash to settle the account within the discount period. What is the amount of cash brought?
    a. $1,000
    b. $2,557
    c. $1,078
    d. None of above

12. Using the information in the previous question, if Stachiw Company paid the account after the discount period, what amount would they send to Smith Company?
    a. $1,078
    b. $1,089
    c. $1,100
    d. None of above

13. The account not impacted by closing entries is:
    a. Salaries expense
    b. Retained earnings
    c. Accumulated depreciation
    d. None of the above

14. For 2015, Smith Corporation reported net income of $36,000 and total service revenue was $900,000. 6,000 shares of common stock were outstanding on January 1, 2015, and 12,000 shares of common stock were outstanding on December 31, 2015. No preferred stock existed during 2015. What were the 2015 earnings per share?
    a. $6.25
    b. $4.00
    c. $3.50
    d. None of the above

15. In early 2015, a company has purchased a tract of land. It expects to build a production plant on the land in approximately 7 years. During the 7 years before construction, the land will be rented to a local farmer. During the seven year period, the land should be reported as:
    a. Land expense
    b. An intangible asset
    c. Long term investment
    d. None of the above

16. On December 2014, the end of Smith Corporation's fiscal period, rent is paid covering the period Jan. 1-June 30, 2015. The correct journal entry to record this transaction would be:
    a. Debit- Prepaid rent, Credit- Cash
    b. Debit- Cash, credit, Credit-Prepaid rent
    c. Debit- Accounts payable, Credit- Prepaid Cash
    d. None of the above

17. The period of time covered by the income statement is the same as period covered by the statement of retained earnings.
    a. True
    b. False

18. A company raising cash by issuing common stock is an example of a(n):
    a. Delivering activity
    b. Financing activity
    c. Operating activity
    d. Investing activity

19. A business owned by one individual is a:
    a. Sole Proprietorship
    b. Government unit
    c. Corporation
    d. Partnership

20. A patent owned by a business would appear in which balance sheet section?
    a. Current assets
    b. Current Liabilities
    c. Intangible assets
    d. Property, Plant, and Equipment

21. Accounts receivable is an example of a revenue account.
    a. True
    b. False

22. Prepaid Insurance would appear in which balance sheet section?
    a. Current assets
    b. Current liabilities
    c. Investments
    d. None of the above

23. A current asset is:
    a. Usually found as a separate classification in the income statement
    b. Expected to be converted to cash or used in the business within a relatively short period of time
    c. An asset which is currently being used to produce a product or service
    d. None of the above

24. Net income equals:
    a. Revenues minus expenses
    b. Revenues plus expenses
    c. Revenues minus dividends declared
    d. None of the above

25. Working Capital:
    a. Is a measure of long-term solvency
    b. Equals current assets divided by current liabilities
    c. Equals current assets minus current liabilities
    d. None of the above

26. The accounting concept which allows equipment to be added to accounts receivable on the balance sheet is the:
    a. Economic entity concept
    b. Monetary unit concept
    c. Full disclosure
    d. None of the above

27. Cash received from customers (for work to be performed in the future) would have no effect net income in the period in which the cash was collected.
    a. True
    b. False

28. In the annual report, where would a reader of financial statements find out if the company's financial statements give a fair depiction of its financial position and operating results in accord with "generally accepted accounting principles?"
    a. Balance Sheet
    b. Income Statement
    c. Auditor's report
    d. None of the above

29. The ending balance of retained earnings appears on the balance sheet.
    a. True
    b. False

30. A net loss will result in:
    a. A decrease in contributed capital
    b. An increase in retained earnings
    c. A decrease in total stockholders' equity
    d. None of the above

31. When a company has performed a service and immediately collected payment for this service, the entry to record this transaction:
    a. Debits cash and credits revenue from services
    b. Debits cash and credits revenue collected in advance
    c. Debits cash and credits accounts payable
    d. All of the above

32. Management could determine the amounts due from customers by examining which ledger account?
    a. Unearned revenue
    b. Service Revenue
    c. Supplies
    d. Accounts Receivable
    e. None of the above

33. The statement of retained earnings would NOT show:
    a. The dividends declared
    b. The balance in Accounts Payable
    c. The retained earnings balance
    d. All of the above

34. A business organization whose legal existence would come to an end with the death of one of the owners.
    a. Funeral home
    b. Partnership
    c. Sole proprietorship
    d. Limited Liability Company (LLC)

35. Ability to effectively analyze the accounting information of different companies because they use the same accounting principles.
    a. Economic Entity
    b. Consistency
    c. Full disclosure
    d. Comparability
    e. None of the above

36. The ability of a company to pay its obligations that are expected to become due within the next year or operating cycle.
    a. Liquidity
    b. Solvency
    c. Free cash flow
    d. None of the above

37. To show how successfully your business performed their operations during a period of time, you would report its revenues and expense on the:
    a. Statement of cash flows
    b. Balance Sheet
    c. Income Statement
    d. None of the above

38. The normal balance of the account, "Accumulated depreciation- equipment" is:
    a. Debit
    b. Credit
    c. Balanced
    d. None of the above

39. If an individual asset is decreased, then:
    a. There could be an equal decrease in stock holder's equity
    b. There could be an equal decrease in another asset
    c. There could be an equal increase in a specific liability
    d. None of the above

40. Retained earnings at the end of the period is equal to:
    a. Retained earnings at the beginning of the period plus net income minus liabilities
    b. Net income
    c. Retained earnings at the beginning of the period minus net loss minus dividends
    d. None of the above

41. Which of the following financial statements contains the assets owned by the company?
    a. Income Statement
    b. Retained Earnings Statement
    c. Balance Sheet
    d. None of the above

42. Murphy Company began the year by issuing $50,000 of common stock for cash and borrowing $20,000. The company recorded revenues of $200,000, expenses of $150,000 and paid dividends of $10,000. What was Murphy's net income for the year?
    a. $45,000
    b. $40,000
    c. $30,000
    d. $50,000
    e. None of the above

43. If a company incurred a net loss during the year and declared no cash dividends, total retained earnings would:
    a. Decrease
    b. Increase
    c. Stay the Same
    d. None of the above

44. The party responsible for prepping financing statements of a corporation is:
    a. The shareholders
    b. Management
    c. The internal revenue service
    d. The external auditor (CPA)

45. The total of the debit column on a trial balance is equal to total assets on the balance sheet.
    a. True
    b. False

46. Which of the following would be classified as a financing activity?
    a. Selling merchandise and being paid in cash
    b. Paying your employees a Salary
    c. Borrowing money from the bank
    d. None of the above

47. An accountant recorded the following journal entry for a payment made on account:

Debit Accounts payable 20,000
Credit Cash 20,000

This would cause the trial balance to be out of balance.
   a. True
   b. False

48. Using the information in 47, this error may cause total assets to be understated.
   a. True
   b. False

Lesson 4: Exercises- FIFO, LIFO, Weighted Average Method, and More!

Use the following information for the month of September to answer questions 1-4.

September	1	Beginning inventory	500 units at $40	$20,000
	7	Purchases	700 units at $35	$24,500
	18	Purchases	200 units at $33	$ 6,600
	22	Purchases	450 units at $30	$13,500
	28	Purchases	350 units at $42	$14,700
			2,200 units	$79,300

The company uses the periodic inventory method and a physical count of merchandise inventory on September 30 reveals there are 1,000 units on hand.

1. Using the LIFO method, the value of ending inventory for September is:
    a. $20,000
    b. $37,500
    c. $16,000
    d. None of the above

2. Using the LIFO method, the amount of cost of goods sold for September is:
    a. $20,000
    b. $16,000
    c. $41,800
    d. None of the above

3. Using the weighted average cost method, the total value of ending inventory is:
    a. $14,420
    b. $19,000
    c. $36,050
    d. None of the above

4. Using the FIFO inventory method, the amount of cost of goods sold is:
    a. $15,000
    b. $18,000
    c. $63,100
    d. None of the above

Cost of goods sold	$225,000
Operating expenses	$45,000
Income tax expense	$10,000
Sales returns and allowances	$9,000
Dividends returned and paid	$5,000
Gross sales (all on credit)	$300,000
Retained earnings, January 1, 2015	$20,000

5. Use the information above for questions 5-7. Net Income for 2015 would be:
   a. $16,000
   b. $11,000
   c. $12,000
   d. None of the above

6. The gross profit margin for 2015 would be:
   a. 25%
   b. 4%
   c. 23%
   d. None of above

7. The ending Retained earnings balance on December 31, 2015:
   a. $91,000
   b. $64,000
   c. $41,000
   d. None of the above

Lesson 5: Multiple Choice Exercises- Managerial Accounting

1. Management functions include:
    a. directing
    b. controlling
    c. planning
    d. all of the above

2. Which of the following does not apply to the content of managerial reports?
    a. Reporting standard is relevant to the decision to be made
    b. Pertain to the entity as a whole and is highly aggregated
    c. Pertain to subunits of the entity and may be very detailed
    d. May extend beyond double entry accounting system

3. If annual overhead costs are expected to be $2,000,000 and 400,000 total labor hours are anticipated (80% direct, 20% indirect), the overhead rate based on director labor hours is?
    a. 5.00
    b. 25.00
    c. 6.25
    d. 4.00

4. Direct materials and direct labor are:
    a. period costs
    b. overhead costs
    c. product costs
    d. indirect costs

5. If activity level increases 25% and a specific cost increases from $40,000 to $50,000, this cost would be classified as a?
    a. mixed cost
    b. variable cost
    c. fixed cost
    d. none of the above

6. A job order sheet includes:
    a. a total when a job is completed and transferred to cost of goods sold
    b. the selling price of the job
    c. all manufacturing overhead costs for the period
    d. all manufacturing costs for a job

7. Machine hours would be an accurate cost driver for:
   a. machine set up costs
   b. inspection costs
   c. machining costs
   d. workers' salaries

8. In a job order cost system, debits to Work in Process Inventory originate from all of the following except?
   a. applying the predetermined overhead rate
   b. assigning direct materials from requisition slips
   c. assigning director labor from time tickets
   d. assigning actual manufacturing overhead costs to jobs

9. If total fixed costs are $750,000 and variable costs as a percentage of unit selling price are 40%, then breakeven point is?
   a. $850,000
   b. $925,000
   c. $1,250,000
   d. $750,000

10. The master budget includes all of the following except:
    a. budgeted income statement
    b. cash budget
    c. budgeted balance sheet
    d. capital expenditure budget

11. Operating leverage refers to the extent to which a company's net income reacts to a given change in:
    a. production
    b. variable costs
    c. sales
    d. overhead costs

12. Which of the following is not a step in preparing a production cost report?
    a. compute equivalent units of production
    b. assign costs to particular jobs
    c. compute the physical unit flow
    d. prepare a cost reconciliation

13. Just in time processing strives to inventories by using a:
    a. just in case approach
    b. push approach
    c. pull approach
    d. process approach

14. A written statement of management's plans for a specified future time period.
    a. accounting plan
    b. research plan
    c. sales budget
    d. budget

15. Controllable fixed costs are deducted from the contribution margin to arrive at:
    a. income statement
    b. controllable balance sheet
    c. controllable margin
    d. realized income

16. If actual overhead is $60,000, and overhead applied is $57,000 and overhead for the standard hours is $68,000, then the overhead controllable variance is?
    a. $5,000 Unfavorable
    b. $3,000 Favorable
    c. $8,000 Favorable
    d. $11,000 Unfavorable

17. An example of qualitative data is:
    a. product cost
    b. customer satisfaction
    c. gross profit
    d. expenses

18. A firm had beginning finished goods inventory of $10,000, ending finished goods inventory of $15,000, and its cost of goods sold was $75,000. The cost of goods manufactured was:
    a. $80,000
    b. $85,000
    c. $75,000
    d. $65,000

19. Cost allocation is the charging of a:
   a. product with the direct labor costs relating to the product
   b. cost center with the overhead costs resulting solely from the existence of the cost center
   c. product with the direct labor and materials costs relating to the product

Lesson 6: Practice Exercises

1. Adjusted trial balance of the Murphy Company included the following selected accounts:

	Debit	Credit
Sales Revenue		$745,000
Sales Returns and Allowances	$ 40,000	
Sales Discounts	19,500	
Cost of Goods Sold	317,000	
Freight-out	8,000	
Advertising Expense	15,000	
Loss on Sale of Equipment	4,000	
Interest Expense	19,000	
Store Salaries Expense	64,000	
Utilities Expense	33,000	
Depreciation Expense	23,500	
Interest Revenue		25,000
Dividends Declared	8,700	

Note: Income Tax Rate is 35%

Compute the following amounts:

    A. Gross Profit

    B. Total Operating Expenses

    C. Net Income

2. Explain why cost flow assumptions (FIFO, LIFO, and Weighted Average) are used by merchandising companies.

3. The account, "Accounts receivable," contains a debit of $8,000. What is the most likely reason this would result in the posting?

4. List two primary contributions a journal makes to recording process.

Lesson 7: Financial Statements

1. Kitty Cleaners began business on June 1, 2010. The trial balance of Kitty Cleaners as of July 1, 2014, is shown below.

	Debit	Credit
Cash	8,000	
Accounts receivable	10,000	
Supplies	9,500	
Short-term investments	5,050	
Accounts payable		1,375
Common stock		32,975
Retained earnings	1,800	
	34,350	34,350

The July transactions were as follows:

July 6 - Collected $8,200 in cash from the June 30 accounts receivable.
  8 - Purchased supplies on account, $355.
  11 - Received $7,545 in cash for services provided.
  14 - Paid creditors $600 of accounts payable.
  17 - Paid employee salaries, $3,750.
  22 - Billed customers for services provided, $922
  28 - Collected service fees in advance, $560
  29 - Paid employee salaries for remainder of July $1,306.
  30 - Received a bill for July utilities of $966.
  30 - Paid $900 for rent (one-third for July and the remainder for August and September)

A. Prepare a general ledger using T accounts. Enter the opening balances in the ledger accounts as of July 1st. You may need to create additional accounts to record transactions.
B. Journalize the transactions
C. Post to the ledger accounts
D. Prepare a trial balance as of July 31st.

Please Show Work Here:

2. The Pounds Company adjusted account balances as of December 31, 2015 are as follows:

Sales	1,300,000
Purchases	800,000
Purchase Discounts	15,000
Purchase Returns and Allowances	1,000
Extraordinary loss, Net of Applicable Taxes of 5,000	15,000
Cash	120,000
Selling Expenses	98,000
Accounts Receivable	50,000
Common Stock	260,000
Accumulated Depreciation	42,000
Pain-in-capital in excess of par	17,000
Inventory, Jan 1st	130,000
Inventory Dec 31st	115,000
Accounts Payable	73,000
Retained Earnings, Jan 1st	67,000
Interest Expense	12,000
General and Administrative Expenses	76,000
Allowance for Doubtful Accounts	2,000
Notes Payable	160,000
Property, Plant, Equipment	140,000
Income Tax Expense	34,000
Dividends Declared and Paid	21,000

Prepare a multi-step income statement.

Answer Key

Lesson 1: Accounting Basics with Vocabulary

Instructions: Match the word with its correct definition.

Exercise 1

1. E. Sarbanes Oxley Act
2. D. Accounting
3. G. Liabilities
4. B. Partnership
5. H. Stockholder's Equity
6. A. Sole Proprietorship
7. C. Corporation
8. F. Assets

Exercise 2

1. E. Accounts Payable
2. D. Accounts Receivable
3. F. Expenses
4. B. Dividends
5. C. Inventory
6. A. Common Stock

Exercise 3

1. F. Management Discussion and Analysis
2. E. Annual Reports
3. B. Retained Earnings Statement
4. A. Income Statements
5. G. Notes
6. H. Auditor's Report
7. C. Balance Sheet
8. D. Statement of Cash Flows

Exercise 4

1. D. Current Liabilities
2. C. Intangible Assets
3. E. Long Term Liabilities
4. A. Current Assets
5. F. Common Stock
6. B. Property, Plant, Equipment

Exercise 5

1. **C. Prepaid Expense**
2. **A. Adjusting Entries**
3. **E. Unearned Revenue**
4. **D. Depreciation**
5. **H. Adjusted Trial Balance**
6. **G. Accrued Expenses**
7. **F. Accrued Revenues**
8. **B. Deferrals**

Exercise 6

1. **C. First In, First Out**
2. **E. Average Cost**
3. **D. Last In, Last Out**
4. **B. Specification Identification Method**
5. **F. Lower Cost or Market**
6. **G. Consigned Goods**
7. **A. Just In Time Inventory**

Exercise 7

1. **G. Premium**
2. **A. Convertible Bonds**
3. **F. Maturity Date**
4. **B. Callable Bonds**
5. **E. Present Value**
6. **D. Face Value**
7. **C. Bond Certificate**

Exercise 8

1. **C. Real Accounts**
2. **E. Ledger**
3. **G. Trial Balance**
4. **D. Nominal Accounts**
5. **F. Journal**
6. **A. Event**
7. **B. Transaction**

Exercise 9

1. F. Non-Controlling Interest
2. A. Operating Section
3. G. Earnings Per Share
4. B. Non-Operating Section
5. C. Income Tax
6. D. Discontinued Operations
7. E. Extraordinary Items

Exercise 10

1. E. Balance Scorecard
2. D. Reengineering
3. B. Product Differentiation
4. F. Unused Capacity
5. G. Downsizing
6. A. Strategy
7. C. Cost Leadership

Exercise 11

1. F. Cost of Goods Sold
2. F. LIFO
3. D. Temporary Accounts
4. J. FIFO
5. A. Interest Revenue
6. I. Days in Inventory
7. B. A Contra Account
8. G. Gross Profit
9. C. Purchase Discount
10. H. Adjusted Trial Balance

Lesson 2: Journal Entries

Instructions: Journalize the transactions.

1. The following transactions in August were as follows:

August 4-Collected $5,670 in cash from May 30th accounts receivable

    Debit Cash $5,670

        Credit Accounts Receivable $5,670

August 5-Received $3,970 in cash for services provided

    Debit Cash $3,970

        Credit Service Revenue $3,970

August 7-Purchased supplies on account for $1,020

    Debit Supplies $1,020

        Credit Accounts Payable $1,020

August 9-Paid employee salaries of $4,480

    Debit Salaries and Wages Expense $4,480

        Credit Cash $4,480

August 12-Paid creditors $2,960 of accounts payable

    Debit Accounts Payable $2,960

        Credit Cash $2,960

August 14-Collected service fees in advance for $1,740

    Debit Cash $1,740

        Credit $1,740

August 17-Received a bill for the utilities for $580

    Debit Utilities Expense $580

        Credit Accounts Payable $580

August 23-Billed customers for services provided for $2,810

    Debit Accounts Receivable $2,810

        Credit Service Revenue $2,810

August 26-Paid $600 for rent (One third covers August and the remainder covers the next two months)

Debit Rent Expense $200

Debit Prepaid Rent $400

Credit Cash $600

August 31-Paid a cash dividend of $990 (First time dividends have been declared)

Debit Dividends Declared $990

Credit Cash $990

2. Nanu Inc. is a furniture retailer and uses the perpetual inventory system. During November, Nanu completed the following merchandising transactions:

Nov. 2 Purchased merchandise on account from Williams Co. $10,700, terms 1/10, n/30
Nov. 4 Sold merchandise on account $16,000, terms 2/10, n/30. The cost of the
   merchandise sold was $8,700.
Nov. 5 Paid freight of $800 on the Nov. 4 sale
Nov. 6 Received credit from Williams Co. for merchandise returned, $1,400 (Nov. 2
   Purchase)
Nov. 11 Paid Williams Co. in full, less the discount

Prepare journal entries on the books of Nanu Inc. to record each of these transactions (only dates necessary, no explanation required).

Nov. 2 Debit Inventory $10,700
Credit Accounts Payable $10,700

Nov. 4 Debit Accounts Receivable $16,000
Credit Revenue $16,000

Nov. 4 Debit Cost of Goods Sold $8,700
Credit Inventory $8,700

Nov. 5 Debit Freight Out $800
Credit Cash $800

Nov. 6 Debit Accounts Payable $1,400
Credit Inventory $1,400

Nov. 11 Debit Accounts Payable $9,300
Credit Cash $9,207
Credit Inventory $93

3. On June 15th 2015, Kevin Smith filed for corporate status in the state of Missouri. The articles authorized 250,000 shares of common stock. The corporation was named 'Smith Inc.' On December 31, 2015, the transactions included the following:

A. On December 14th, an investor bought 500 shares of common stock for $100,000.

Debit Cash $100,000

Credit Common Stock $100,000

B. On December 19th, Kevin Smith purchased a van for his family. The cost of the car was $26,789 and the license, taxes, etc. were $934. He paid cash for all these items.

No entry required (Was not a company transaction)

C. On December 29th, Smith arranged a loan by issuing a note for $60,000, with a requirement that the money was to be transferred to Smith's account early on December 31st. Smith was required to pay $400 a month interest (due on the last day of each month starting next year) and the $60,000 was to be paid off by December 31, 2016.

Debit Cash $60,000

Credit Notes Payable $60,000

D. On December 31, Smith Inc. paid $139,000 to its manufacturer for devices that were delivered the same day. These inventory items will be sold to distributors in the future.

Debit Inventory $139,000

Credit Cash $139,000

4. The Williams Corporation is a well-established company. The following transactions took place in March 2015.

A. Williams Corporation sold $378,000 worth of merchandise during the month. Of this amount, $261,000 was received in cash and the remainder on account.

Debit Cash $261,000

Debit Accounts Receivable $117,000

Credit Sales $378,000

B. Williams incurred expenses of $30,189 that related to selling, general, and administrative items. Of these, $18,022 was paid in cash and the remainder on account.

Debit Expenses $30,189

    Credit Cash $18,022

    Credit Accounts payable $12,167

C. Williams paid dividends of $6,034 to the shareholders.

Debit Dividends $6,034

    Credit Cash $6,034

D. Williams paid cash of $123,004 to its research and development consultants for a new product under consideration. This transaction is considered as an R&D transaction.

Debit Expense $123,004

    Credit Cash $123,004

5. Dar Inc. exchanged old equipment and $10,000 cash for equipment owned by Kitty Inc.

Below is information about the asset exchanged by Dar Inc. Assume the transaction has commercial substance. Journalize this transaction.

	Cost	Accumulated Dep.	Book Value	Fair Value
Dar's Equipment	$250,000	$150,000	$100,000	$105,000

    Debit Equipment $115,000 (Fair value + cash)

    Debit Accumulated Depreciation $150,000

        Credit Equipment $250,000

        Credit Cash $10,000

        Credit Gain on Exchange $5,000

6. The Zuehlke Company was incorporated on January 1, 2014 with an initial capital of 10,000 shares of common stock having a $15 par value. The following transactions took place in January:

January 2: Office supplies costing $3,509 were purchased on account

Debit Supplies $3,509

Credit Accounts Payable $3,509

January 3: $18,000 was paid as an advance for three months' rent

Debit Prepaid Rent $18,000

Credit Cash $18,000

January 7: Provided services to its customers and received $28,000 in cash

Debit Cash $28,000

Credit Service Revenue $28,000

January 11: Received $15,000 as an advance payment from customers

Debit Cash $15,000

Credit Unearned Revenue $15,000

January 17: Paid wages to its employees for $3900

Debit Wages Expense $3,900

Credit Cash $3,900

January 22: Received telephone bill of $844

Debit Telephone Expense $844

Credit Utilities Payable $844

7. We are following Mike around for the first few months as he starts his barbecue food chain called "Mike's Barbecue." Here are the events that took place.

On January 1th, Mike finds a nice building to put his restaurant in and signs a lease for $600 a month.

No entry required

On January 8th, Mike takes out a loan to renovate his restaurant for $75,000 and agrees to pay back $1,000 a month. He spends the entire loan on improving the building's looks.

Debit Leasehold Improvements $75,000

Credit Accounts Payable $75,000

On January 11th, Mike buys $2,000 worth of supplies on account from vendors. He agrees to pay $250 a month.

Debit Inventory $2,000

Credit Accounts Payable $2,000

On January 25th, the store opens up for business. In 5 days, Mike makes $15,020 in sales.

Debit Cash $15,020

Credit Sales Revenue $15,020

On February 1st, Mike's first rent payment is due.

Debit Rent Expense $600

Credit Cash $600

On February 6th, Mike pays his employees $2,098 for their work.

Debit Wages Expense $2,098

Credit Cash $2,098

On February 8th, Mike pays for an electric bill costing $340 and his first payment from his January 8th loan is also due.

Debit Utility Expense $340

Credit Cash $340

Debit Accounts Payable $1,000

Credit Cash $1,000

On February 11th, Mike's first vendor inventory payment is due.

Debit Accounts Payable $250

Credit cash $250

Lesson 3: Multiple Choice and True/False On Basic Material

1. A company pays for inventory within the cash discount period and receives the discount. This action will increase the gross profit percentage on these units when they are sold.
   a. **True**
   b. False

Use the following information for questions 2 to 4: Stachiw Corporation (whose fiscal year ends on December 31) signed a 1 year note payable in the amount of $8000 on October 1, 2015. The note requires interest at an annual rate of 6%, principal and interest to be paid on the maturity date (November 30, 2016).

2. The amount of interest accrued on December 31, 2015 on the books of Stachiw Corp. is:
   a. $320
   b. $120
   c. $480
   d. **$120**

3. The adjusting entry for this accrued interest on the books of Stachiw Corp. on December 31, 2015 would be:
   a. **Debit: Interest expense and Credit: Interest payable**
   b. Debit: Interest receivable and Credit: Interest revenue
   c. Debit: Note payable and Credit: Cash
   d. Debit: Interest payable and Credit: Interest revenue

4. The correct entry on the books of Stachiw Corp. on October 1, 2015 would:
   a. Increase net income
   b. Decrease net income
   c. Decrease total assets
   d. **Have no effect total income**
   e. All of the above

5. The payment of a pre-existing accounts payable:
   a. Increases net income
   b. Decreases net income
   c. **Has no effect on net income**
   d. All of the above

6. On the income statement for a service business (such as an advertising agency), an amount referred to as gross profit would not be reported.
   a. **True**
   b. False

7. The Cook Apartments, Inc. collected one year of rent in advance on May 1, 2015 totaling $9,000 and recorded the collection as a liability. If their fiscal year ends on December 31, the revenue to be reported for 2015 would be:
   a. $5,600
   b. **$6,000**
   c. None of the above

8. Goods are shipped by the Williams Company on December 16, 2015, FOB destination. These goods are received by Williams' customer December 26, 2015. The goods should be included in Williams' ending inventory on December 31, 2015.
   a. True
   b. **False**

9. Stachiw's Dry Cleaners follows the revenue recognition principle. On October 4 a customer drops off laundry for cleaning. The cleaning is completed on October 7. On November 1 the customer picks up the clothing. When should Stachiw show that the revenue was earned?
   a. October 4
   b. **October 7**
   c. November 1
   d. None of the above

10. On March 1, 2015, Smith Corporation paid $48,000 cash for equipment that will be used in business operations. The equipment will be used for four years. Smith records depreciation expense of $9,000 for the calendar year ending December 31, 2015. Which accounting principle has been violated?
    a. Matching principle
    b. Depreciation principle
    c. Expense recognition principle
    d. **No principle has been violated**

11. Smith Company sells merchandise on account for $1,500 to Stachiw Company with credit terms of 2/10, n/30. Stachiw Company returns $400 of merchandise that was damaged, along with cash to settle the account within the discount period. What is the amount of cash brought?
    a. $1,000
    b. $2,557
    c. $1,078
    d. None of above

12. Using the information in the previous question, if Stachiw Company paid the account after the discount period, what amount would they send to Smith Company?
    a. $1,078
    b. $1,089
    c. $1,100
    d. None of above

13. The account not impacted by closing entries is:
    a. Salaries expense
    b. Retained earnings
    c. Accumulated depreciation
    d. None of the above

14. For 2015, Smith Corporation reported net income of $36,000 and total service revenue was $900,000. 6,000 shares of common stock were outstanding on January 1, 2015, and 12,000 shares of common stock were outstanding on December 31, 2015. No preferred stock existed during 2015. What were the 2015 earnings per share?
    a. $6.25
    b. $4.00
    c. $3.50
    d. None of the above

15. In early 2015, a company has purchased a tract of land. It expects to build a production plant on the land in approximately 7 years. During the 7 years before construction, the land will be rented to a local farmer. During the seven year period, the land should be reported as:
    a. Land expense
    b. An intangible asset
    c. Long term investment
    d. None of the above

16. On December 2014, the end of Smith Corporation's fiscal period, rent is paid covering the period Jan. 1-June 30, 2015. The correct journal entry to record this transaction would be:
    a. **Debit- Prepaid rent, Credit- Cash**
    b. Debit- Cash, credit, Credit-Prepaid rent
    c. Debit- Accounts payable, Credit- Prepaid Cash
    d. None of the above

17. The period of time covered by the income statement is the same as period covered by the statement of retained earnings.
    a. **True**
    b. False

18. A company raising cash by issuing common stock is an example of a(n):
    a. Delivering activity
    b. **Financing activity**
    c. Operating activity
    d. Investing activity

19. A business owned by one individual is a:
    a. **Sole Proprietorship**
    b. Government unit
    c. Corporation
    d. Partnership

20. A patent owned by a business would appear in which balance sheet section?
    a. Current assets
    b. Current Liabilities
    c. **Intangible assets**
    d. Property, Plant, and Equipment

21. Accounts receivable is an example of a revenue account.
    a. True
    b. **False**

22. Prepaid Insurance would appear in which balance sheet section?
    a. **Current assets**
    b. Current liabilities
    c. Investments
    d. None of the above

23. A current asset is:
    a. Usually found as a separate classification in the income statement
    b. **Expected to be converted to cash or used in the business within a relatively short period of time**
    c. An asset which is currently being used to produce a product or service
    d. None of the above

24. Net income equals:
    a. **Revenues minus expenses**
    b. Revenues plus expenses
    c. Revenues minus dividends declared
    d. None of the above

25. Working Capital:
    a. Is a measure of long-term solvency
    b. Equals current assets divided by current liabilities
    c. **Equals current assets minus current liabilities**
    d. None of the above

26. The accounting concept which allows equipment to be added to accounts receivable on the balance sheet is the:
    a. Economic entity concept
    b. **Monetary unit concept**
    c. Full disclosure
    d. None of the above

27. Cash received from customers (for work to be performed in the future) would have no effect net income in the period in which the cash was collected.
    a. **True**
    b. False

28. In the annual report, where would a reader of financial statements find out if the company's financial statements give a fair depiction of its financial position and operating results in accord with "generally accepted accounting principles?"
    a. Balance Sheet
    b. Income Statement
    c. Auditor's report
    d. None of the above

29. The ending balance of retained earnings appears on the balance sheet.
    a. True
    b. False

30. A net loss will result in:
    a. A decrease in contributed capital
    b. An increase in retained earnings
    c. A decrease in total stockholders' equity
    d. None of the above

31. When a company has performed a service and immediately collected payment for this service, the entry to record this transaction:
    a. Debits cash and credits revenue from services
    b. Debits cash and credits revenue collected in advance
    c. Debits cash and credits accounts payable
    d. All of the above

32. Management could determine the amounts due from customers by examining which ledger account?
    a. Unearned revenue
    b. Service Revenue
    c. Supplies
    d. Accounts Receivable
    e. None of the above

33. The statement of retained earnings would NOT show:
    a. The dividends declared
    b. The balance in Accounts Payable
    c. The retained earnings balance
    d. All of the above

34. A business organization whose legal existence would come to an end with the death of one of the owners.
    a. Funeral home
    b. Partnership
    c. Sole proprietorship
    d. Limited Liability Company (LLC)

35. Ability to effectively analyze the accounting information of different companies because they use the same accounting principles.
    a. Economic Entity
    b. Consistency
    c. Full disclosure
    d. Comparability
    e. None of the above

36. The ability of a company to pay its obligations that are expected to become due within the next year or operating cycle.
    a. Liquidity
    b. Solvency
    c. Free cash flow
    d. None of the above

37. To show how successfully your business performed their operations during a period of time, you would report its revenues and expense on the:
    a. Statement of cash flows
    b. Balance Sheet
    c. Income Statement
    d. None of the above

38. The normal balance of the account, "Accumulated depreciation- equipment" is:
    a. Debit
    b. Credit
    c. Balanced
    d. None of the above

39. If an individual asset is decreased, then:
    a. There could be an equal decrease in stock holder's equity
    b. There could be an equal decrease in another asset
    c. There could be an equal increase in a specific liability
    d. None of the above

40. Retained earnings at the end of the period is equal to:
    a. Retained earnings at the beginning of the period plus net income minus liabilities
    b. Net income
    c. **Retained earnings at the beginning of the period minus net loss minus dividends**
    d. None of the above

41. Which of the following financial statements contains the assets owned by the company?
    a. Income Statement
    b. Retained Earnings Statement
    c. **Balance Sheet**
    d. None of the above

42. Murphy Company began the year by issuing $50,000 of common stock for cash and borrowing $20,000. The company recorded revenues of $200,000, expenses of $150,000 and paid dividends of $10,000. What was Murphy's net income for the year?
    a. $45,000
    b. $40,000
    c. $30,000
    d. **$50,000**
    e. None of the above

43. If a company incurred a net loss during the year and declared no cash dividends, total retained earnings would:
    a. **Decrease**
    b. Increase
    c. Stay the Same
    d. None of the above

44. The party responsible for prepping financing statements of a corporation is:
    a. The shareholders
    b. **Management**
    c. The internal revenue service
    d. The external auditor (CPA)

45. The total of the debit column on a trial balance is equal to total assets on the balance sheet.
    a. True
    b. **False**

46. Which of the following would be classified as a financing activity?
   a. Selling merchandise and being paid in cash
   b. Paying your employees a Salary
   c. Borrowing money from the bank
   d. None of the above

47. An accountant recorded the following journal entry for a payment made on account:

   Debit Accounts payable 20,000
   　　　　　　　　　　　　Credit Cash 20,000

   This would cause the trial balance to be out of balance.
   a. True
   b. False

48. Using the information in 47, this error may cause total assets to be understated.
   a. True
   b. False

Lesson 4: Exercises- FIFO, LIFO, Weighted Average Method, and More!

Use the following information for the month of September to answer questions 1-4.

September	1	Beginning inventory	500 units at $40	$20,000
	7	Purchases	700 units at $35	$24,500
	18	Purchases	200 units at $33	$ 6,600
	22	Purchases	450 units at $30	$13,500
	28	Purchases	350 units at $42	$14,700
			2,200 units	$79,300

The company uses the periodic inventory method and a physical count of merchandise inventory on September 30 reveals there are 1,000 units on hand.

1. Using the LIFO method, the value of ending inventory for September is:
   a. $20,000
   b. $37,500
   c. $16,000
   d. None of the above

2. Using the LIFO method, the amount of cost of goods sold for September is:
   a. $20,000
   b. $16,000
   c. $41,800
   d. None of the above

3. Using the weighted average cost method, the total value of ending inventory is:
   a. $14,420
   b. $19,000
   c. $36,050
   d. None of the above

4. Using the FIFO inventory method, the amount of cost of goods sold is:
   a. $15,000
   b. $18,000
   c. $63,100
   d. None of the above

Cost of goods sold	$225,000
Operating expenses	$45,000
Income tax expense	$10,000
Sales returns and allowances	$9,000
Dividends returned and paid	$5,000
Gross sales (all on credit)	$300,000
Retained earnings, January 1, 2015	$20,000

5. Use the information above for questions 5-7. Net Income for 2015 would be:
    a. $16,000
    b. **$11,000**
    c. $12,000
    d. None of the above

6. The gross profit margin for 2015 would be:
    a. 25%
    b. 4%
    c. **23%**
    d. None of above

7. The ending Retained earnings balance on December 31, 2015:
    a. $91,000
    b. $64,000
    c. $41,000
    d. **None of the above**

Lesson 5: Multiple Choice Exercises- Managerial Accounting

1. Management functions include:
   a. directing
   b. controlling
   c. planning
   d. all of the above

2. Which of the following does not apply to the content of managerial reports?
   a. Reporting standard is relevant to the decision to be made
   b. Pertain to the entity as a whole and is highly aggregated
   c. Pertain to subunits of the entity and may be very detailed
   d. May extend beyond double entry accounting system

3. If annual overhead costs are expected to be $2,000,000 and 400,000 total labor hours are anticipated (80% direct, 20% indirect), the overhead rate based on director labor hours is?
   a. 5.00
   b. 25.00
   c. 6.25
   d. 4.00

4. Direct materials and direct labor are:
   a. period costs
   b. overhead costs
   c. product costs
   d. indirect costs

5. If activity level increases 25% and a specific cost increases from $40,000 to $50,000, this cost would be classified as a?
   a. mixed cost
   b. variable cost
   c. fixed cost
   d. none of the above

6. A job order sheet includes:
   a. a total when a job is completed and transferred to cost of goods sold
   b. the selling price of the job
   c. all manufacturing overhead costs for the period
   d. all manufacturing costs for a job

7. Machine hours would be an accurate cost driver for:
   a. machine set up costs
   b. inspection costs
   c. machining costs
   d. workers' salaries

8. In a job order cost system, debits to Work in Process Inventory originate from all of the following except?
   a. applying the predetermined overhead rate
   b. assigning direct materials from requisition slips
   c. assigning director labor from time tickets
   d. assigning actual manufacturing overhead costs to jobs

9. If total fixed costs are $750,000 and variable costs as a percentage of unit selling price are 40%, then breakeven point is?
   a. $850,000
   b. $925,000
   c. $1,250,000
   d. $750,000

10. The master budget includes all of the following except:
    a. budgeted income statement
    b. cash budget
    c. budgeted balance sheet
    d. capital expenditure budget

11. Operating leverage refers to the extent to which a company's net income reacts to a given change in:
    a. production
    b. variable costs
    c. sales
    d. overhead costs

12. Which of the following is not a step in preparing a production cost report?
    a. compute equivalent units of production
    b. assign costs to particular jobs
    c. compute the physical unit flow
    d. prepare a cost reconciliation

13. Just in time processing strives to inventories by using a:
    a. just in case approach
    b. push approach
    c. pull approach
    d. process approach

14. A written statement of management's plans for a specified future time period.
    a. accounting plan
    b. research plan
    c. sales budget
    d. budget

15. Controllable fixed costs are deducted from the contribution margin to arrive at:
    a. income statement
    b. controllable balance sheet
    c. controllable margin
    d. realized income

16. If actual overhead is $60,000, and overhead applied is $57,000 and overhead for the standard hours is $68,000, then the overhead controllable variance is?
    a. $5,000 Unfavorable
    b. $3,000 Favorable
    c. $8,000 Favorable
    d. $11,000 Unfavorable

17. An example of qualitative data is:
    a. product cost
    b. customer satisfaction
    c. gross profit
    d. expenses

18. A firm had beginning finished goods inventory of $10,000, ending finished goods inventory of $15,000, and its cost of goods sold was $75,000. The cost of goods manufactured was:
    a. $80,000
    b. $85,000
    c. $75,000
    d. $65,000

19. Cost allocation is the charging of a:
    a. product with the direct labor costs relating to the product
    b. **cost center with the overhead costs resulting solely from the existence of the cost center**
    c. product with the direct labor and materials costs relating to the product

Lesson 6: Practice Exercises

1. Adjusted trial balance of the Murphy Company included the following selected accounts:

	Debit	Credit
Sales Revenue		$745,000
Sales Returns and Allowances	$ 40,000	
Sales Discounts	19,500	
Cost of Goods Sold	317,000	
Freight-out	8,000	
Advertising Expense	15,000	
Loss on Sale of Equipment	4,000	
Interest Expense	19,000	
Store Salaries Expense	64,000	
Utilities Expense	33,000	
Depreciation Expense	23,500	
Interest Revenue		25,000
Dividends Declared	8,700	

Note: Income Tax Rate is 35%

Compute the following amounts:

- A Gross Profit
    - a. **$368,500**
        - i. **Hint: Gross Profit = Net Sales-COGS**
- B. Total Operating Expenses
    - a. **$143,500**
        - i. **Hint: Add up your expenses**
        - ii. **Hint: Interest expense should not be included**
- C. Net Income
    - a. **$147,225**
        - i. **Hint: Recall the Income Tax Rate is 35%**

2. Explain why cost flow assumptions (FIFO, LIFO, and Weighted average) are used by merchandising companies.

FIFO, LIFO, and Weighted average are used by merchandising companies because it is easier for companies to use than perpetual inventory. Perpetual inventory takes time and money, while the cost of flow assumptions are more manageable. FIFO and LIFO each have their own advantages such as LIFO having a lower tax expense during times of rising prices.

3. The account, "Accounts receivable," contains a debit of $8,000. What is the most likely reason this would result in the posting?

The most likely transaction was that a company performed a service that but has not yet been paid. Accounts receivable, an asset, would be debited and revenues would not be credited because it increases retained earnings.

4. List two primary contributions a journal makes to the recording process.

1) Lists the transactions in chronological order, making it easier to locate transactions
2) The journal is a way of analyzing transactions by listing them in either debit or credit columns
3) If there is an error in the trial balance, it is easy to go through each transaction in the journal to locate errors

Lesson 7: Financial Statements

1. Kitty Cleaners began business on June 1, 2010. The trial balance of Kitty Cleaners, as of July 1, 2014, is shown below.

	Debit	Credit
Cash	8,000	
Accounts receivable	10,000	
Supplies	9,500	
Short-term investments	5,050	
Accounts payable		1,375
Common stock		32,975
Retained earnings	1,800	
	34,350	34,350

The July transactions were as follows:

July 6 - Collected $8,200 in cash from the June 30 accounts receivable.
      8 - Purchased supplies on account, $355.
      11 - Received $7,545 in cash for services provided.
      14 - Paid creditors $600 of accounts payable.
      17 - Paid employee salaries, $3,750.
      22 - Billed customers for services provided, $922
      28 - Collected service fees in advance, $560
      29 - Paid employee salaries for remainder of July $1,306.
      30 - Received a bill for July utilities of $966.
      30 - Paid $900 for rent (one-third for July and the remainder for August and September)

A. Prepare a general ledger using T accounts. Enter the opening balances in the ledger accounts as of July 1st. You may need to create additional accounts to record transactions.
B. Journalize the transactions
C. Post to the ledger accounts
D. Prepare a trial balance as of July 31st.

Answers to A and C.

Cash	
July 1: 8,000	July 14: 600
July 6: 8,200	July 17: 3,750
July 11: 7,545	July 29: 1,306
July 28: 560	
	July 30: 900
	July 31: 850
Balance: **$16,899**	

Accounts Receivable	
July 1: 10,000	July 8: 8,200
July 22: 922	
Balance: **$2,722**	

Supplies	
July 1: 9,500	
July 9: 355	
Balance: **$9,855**	

Unearned Service Revenue	
	July 1: 0
	July 28: 560
	Balance: **$560**

Prepaid Rent	
July 1: 0	
July 30: 600	
Balance: **$600**	

Retained earnings	
July 1: 1,800	
Balance: **$1,800**	

Salaries and Wages Expense	
July 1: 0	
July 17: 3,750	
July 30: 1,306	
Balance: **$5,056**	

Short-term investments	
July 1: 5,050	
Balance: **$5,050**	

Accounts payable	
July 14: 600	July 1: $1,375
	July 9: 355
	July 30: 966
	Balance: **$2,096**

Common stock	
	July 1: 32,975
	Balance: **$32,975**

Utilities Expense	
July 1: 0	
July 30: 966	
Balance: $966	

Service Revenue	
	July 1: 0
	July 11: 7,545
	July 22: 922
	Balance: $8,467

Dividends	
July 1: 0	
July 31: 850	
Balance: $850	

Rent Expense	
July 1: 0	
July 30: 300	
Balance: $300	

Answer to B.

Date	Transactions		Debit	Credit
	Kitty Cleaners			
	General Journal			
2014	Cash		$ 8,200	
6-Jul	Accounts Receivable			$ 8,200
	(Collected from the June 30)			
	Supplies		$ 355	
8-Jul	Accounts Payable			$ 355
	(Supplies purchases on account)			
	Cash		$ 7,545	
11-Jul	Service Revenue			$ 7,545
	(Received Cash for services)			
	Accounts Payable		$ 600	
14-Jul	Cash			$ 600
	(Paying off money due)			
	Salaries and Wages Expense		$ 3,750	
17-Jul	Cash			$ 3,750
	(Paid off employee salaries)			
	Accounts Receivable		$ 922	
22-Jul	Service Revenue			$ 922
	(Billed customers for services)			
	Cash		$ 560	
28-Jul	Unearned Service Rev.			$ 560
	(Billed service fees in advance)			
	Salaries and Wages Expense		$ 1,306	
29-Jul	Cash			$ 1,306
	(Paid off employee salaries)			
	Utilities Expense		$ 966	
30-Jul	Accountspayable			$ 966
	(Received Bill for July Utilities)			
	Rent Expense		$ 300	
30-Jul	Prepaid Rent		$ 600	
	Cash			$ 900
	(Paid off Jul rent and paid 2 months adv)			
31-Jul	Dividend		$ 850	
	Cash			$ 850

62

Answer to D.

Kitty Cleaners Trial Balance 31-Jul-14	Debit	Credit
Cash	$ 16,899	
Accounts Receivable	$ 2,722	
Supplies	$ 9,855	
Short Term Investment	$ 5,050	
Prepaid Rent	$ 600	
Accounts Payable		$ 2,096
Unearned Service Rev		$ 560
Common Stock		$ 32,975
Utilities Expense	$ 966	
Dividends Declared	$ 850	
Service Rev		$ 8,467
Retained Earnings	$ 1,800	
Rent Expense	$ 300	
Salaries and Wage Expense	$ 5,056	
	$ 44,098	$ 44,098

2. The Pounds Company adjusted account balances as of December 31, 2015 are as follows:

Sales	1,300,000
Purchases	800,000
Purchase Discounts	15,000
Purchase Returns and Allowances	1,000
Extraordinary loss, Net of Applicable Taxes of 5,000	15,000
Cash	120,000
Selling Expenses	98,000
Accounts Receivable	50,000
Common Stock	260,000
Accumulated Depreciation	42,000
Pain-in-capital in excess of par	17,000
Inventory, Jan 1st	130,000
Inventory Dec 31st	115,000
Accounts Payable	73,000
Retained Earnings, Jan 1st	67,000
Interest Expense	12,000
General and Administrative Expenses	76,000
Allowance for Doubtful Accounts	2,000
Notes Payable	160,000
Property, Plant, Equipment	140,000
Income Tax Expense	34,000
Dividends Declared and Paid	21,000

Prepare a multi-step income statement.

		Pounds Company									
		Income Statement									
		For the Year Ended December 31, 2015									
Sales										$	1,300,000
Cost of Goods Sold:											
	Beg Inventory					$	130,000				
	Purchases		$	800,000							
	Purchase Discounts		$	(15,000)							
	Purchase returns and allowances		$	(2,000)							
	Net Purchases					$	783,000				
	Goods Available for sale					$	913,000				
	Ending inventory					$	(115,000)				
	Cost of goods sold									$	798,000
Gross Profit										$	502,000
Operating Expenses:											
	Selling Expenses					$	98,000				
	General and administrative expenses					$	76,000				
	Total Operating expenses									$	174,000
Operating income										$	328,000
Other income (expense):											
	Interest Expense									$	(12,000)
Income before taxes										$	316,000
Income taxes										$	(34,000)
Income before extraordinary items										$	282,000
Extraordinary loss, net of applicable taxes of 5,000										$	(10,000)
Net Income										$	272,000

About the Book

With multiple choice questions, journal entries, and financial statement preparations, this book will help you excel at the basic concepts of accounting.

About the Authors

Jackie Stachiw and Brandon Williams are currently studying Accounting at Saint Louis University. Their excitement and love for this field has given them the inspiration to help others love Accounting too.